T0374009

For David

*New beginnings are often disguised as painful endings*

Lao Tzu

To order additional copies of this book, contact:
Xlibris
1-800-455-039
www.xlibris.com.au
Orders@Xlibris.com.au

# Acceptance

caring for others, caring for ourselves

## Maureen Cochram

# Preface

Some years ago my son David was assaulted and sustained brain injury.
During surgery to remove a blood clot in his brain an inoperable cyst was
discovered and as a result of trauma he developed psoriatic arthritis.

He lost his health, partner, job and lifestyle and came to live with me.

This was the beginning of profound change for both of us.

At times the going has been tough with spiraling
pain, despair and frustration.

I began writing poetry as a form of release and solace
as we both adjusted to a new lifestyle.

While these poems started out as my solo, emerging duets
of differing proportions gave voice to both of us.

As I shared these poems with David something started to shift.
While we were both on a different journey we were moving,
in our own way towards compassionate Acceptance.

He chose the title for this book and encouraged me to have
it published to support people in similar circumstances.

*'Life is not about simply braving the storm*
*It's about learning to dance in the rain'*
Anon

*A little light —*

*contrasted with darkness*

from the dark silent corner he turned
he spoke appreciation
'I like your painting'
his pain drawn eyes lingered on the light
I left it there on the cupboard
a little light so quiet
it's just there on the cupboard
a calm little light contrasted with his darkness
he said without saying
all he really wants
is for someone to be quietly, gently shining a small light
as he journey's through the dark night
a little candle in the window
no more, no less
I'll leave the painting on the cupboard

*Without the dark*
*the stars do not shine so bright*
*(inspired by the colour Indigo)*

please stop the bells
please pull the blinds
please still the noise
please stop the chimes
don't chop those carrots
don't walk on heels
don't turn on the fans
don't drop those pans
please pull the curtains
please close the doors
dark silence, dark silence please
the noise of my pain, the noise in my head, the noise of my fear
retreats in dark silence
your light, your colour, your songs, your voice
intrude on my dark silence
it jars and startles and glares in my face
I seek comfort in a deep dark place
embrace dark silence
to enhance your light
I'm embracing resistance to put up a good fight
please turn off the light
embrace dark silence in this space
for your light to shine brighter
in a bigger place

## Resistance

sometimes I rage
sometimes I wail
why? why? why?
I stomp in the sand and scream to the gulls
the rain and my tears storm down in buckets
why? why? why?
I can't take much more
I'm churning inside
I've tried and I've tried
it's not fair I yell
why, why, why
I wish the pain and the rain would go

## Caring is not a one way street

who says I don't care
it's enough to live with this pain
without being
cornered into guilt again
who says I don't care
I'm aware
I care
I'm off to dads to give you a break

## Spinning and turning

you shut down
you don't talk
your smile has gone
your song unsung
your laugh silenced
your tears unwrung
locked away in tight balls of pain
spinning and spinning again and again
when you seep deep with grief
of lost dreams, hopes and schemes
all doors locked tight
the key rusted and brown
I spin and I spin around and around
where do I turn?
when you silently be
sitting and eating and watching tv
where do I turn?
when the tide overwhelms
I leap out of doors
and shout to the sky
I go with the wind, the tide and the shore
I fly with the gulls
I soar

## Big man/little car

I have a little car
it used to be my mum's
thank god I can still drive it
though my fingers look like thumbs
it's my only means of freedom
and it zips me here and there
I'm grateful for my little car
and the little things we share
driving in the sunshine
by the ocean blue
windows down and a fresh sea breeze
the long horizon view
it takes me to the doctors
the specialist in town
the physio for treatment
it never lets me down
while macho boys need macho toys
she never lets me down
so what if I'm a big man
it's how I feel inside
I'm grateful for this little car
she's taught me so much more
enjoy the journey and the moment
'cause who knows what's in store

## At tention

look at those birds he said
as pelicans circled overhead
they sat and looked

don't push yourself so much he said
as she raced out the door
he sat and looked

at sunset he reminded her to pause
to see a rose pink sky
the gold dipping sun
they sat and looked

at dawn he drew her attention
to puffy clouds and golden light
they stood and looked

he apologised for being a nuisance

## A time to weep

yesterday he walked through the school gate
his first day
he didn't want his mum in class with him
at the corner of the street
she gave into a weep
he wouldn't want her crying like a sook at school

yesterday he struggled wracked with pain
his first day
he didn't want his mum in hospital with him
at the corner of the street
she gave into a weep
he wouldn't want her crying like a sook at hospital

40 years between the scenes
school of life
by any means

## Living like a man

tough being a man living with mum
tough with no money, no friends and no fun
tough being a man living with mum
it's hard when a man can't play
even if I met a woman and reached out for more
what a challenge coming through your door
living like a man on my terms I long to be
living like a man with a job and a woman to love
oh what I'd give
to live on my terms
it rocks my socks when I see those guys with constant
greedy eyes
if only they knew how much they have
so I'm living like a man with my mum
the sum of it all
I simply am
going to ground

## Dark energy

black fog
seeping, creeping bleak surge
your bed of despair
into every nook and cranny
filling the house with the soot of fears
dark heavy energy
I gasp for air

# Doing the self-pity stuff

it's ok to do self-pity once in a while
you can't be expected to keep up the smile
walking on water takes its toll
it's ok to roll in the mud
to wallow and sob and feel a right dud
you're tough and you're strong
you're there for it all
the short and the long
self-pity is shitty if it goes on and on
but get this straight
an occasional outburst is a fine state
like a storm in the night
it settles the dust
it clears all the 'musts'
into the murk, the muck and the wallows
to rise up again to walk in the shallows
with the sun on your back
bouncing back

# Listen

I call her
she listens
she listens to shafting sobs of frustration
she listens
she listens with an open heart
she listens
she listens and I hear

## As good as it gets

what's the gain in all this pain?
asking myself again
I surrender to this pain
I am open to giving with this pain
with little acts of kindness for my mum and dad
perhaps as good as it gets
I have a story
but that's not who I am
it's just a story
it's sort of like spam
even in the murky stash of all the pain and loss
I know I'm more
I'm me at the core
right now I am
that's good

## Treasure in the ruins

walls eroded to dust
seared by the sun
tasted by rain
wind blasted
a smudge on a crop scraped bare
hearth and heart
lighter with love
grounded in welcoming earth

## It's my monkey

some people steal my monkey
they play the drama out
why do they steal my monkey?
I don't want much
simply acknowledge me
be there for me occasionally
some make it their pain
some their excuse
some feed off the issues
that's abuse
some always know someone who's had it worse
some can't cope with knowing
stealing my monkey is a curse
your voyeuristic tendencies
don't help me heal
give me back my monkey
get on with your life
I'm into it big time and that's enough strife

## It's my dance

I love to dance
I love to sing
I love the music
I love the light
it's hell for you
too loud too strong
I pause for one last song

## Compensation

body sucks
brain scrambled
emotions storming
head tumbled
broken record messages again and again
persona stripped
ego churning
unlocking my heart
beginning to gnaw
beginning to thaw
pulsing crimson in a dark space

## Frayed daze —
## frayed days

walking half asleep
slow rumblings
tormented slumber
numb, numb, number
you totter from your room
struggling in a velcrose haze
you teeter round the edges of your frayed daze
I teeter round the edges of my frayed days

## Knock at the door

you opened the door
now they come back for more
I can't open the door
my pain is my world

## The cure

eyes glazed pain pools drained of light
body cramped and screwed up tight
the shutting down, the seizing up
we can fix it they said
the thing in your head
your body twisted in pain
the pain
the brain
all your ills
this month a 100 pills
then the pills to fix the ills of the pills
we'll stop it they said
we'll fix it they said
they did
now he's living and dead
dead asleep in the bed
thank god for modern medicine

## Like a bird

dark clouds
screaming for attention
intoxicating freedom
cruising higher, higher
soaring through my pain
like a bird I long to fly

## Self-sabotage

I listened to what you thought I should do
I know you were trying to help
I did what you wanted
to ease your pain
now I'm in more pain
I sabotaged myself
I won't do that again


## If you can find a laugh
## you can find a light

well now it's like this he said
they found a thing in my brain
don't know what it is but they measured it
in a few months they'll measure it again
it's big
well it's like this he said
the stuff that's seizing up my body
the curling toes and locked knees
no cure
the pain is level ten – pills please
well it's like this he said
with a laugh in the dark
gee, it's a good thing I've got a big head
with a laugh in the dark
gee, brain squashed, body squeezed
how come I'm so brilliant and beautiful – geeze!

## Indulging in distractions 'cause I can

how can you complain about the rain
when he's in so much pain
how can you complain about the bills
when he's riddled with so many ills
how can you grizzle about your cakes
when his body is full of constant aches
how can you grump about the mess
when he's chocked up with distress
how can you moan about the cold
when he's so desperate to grow old
it's easier to focus on stuff
than face reality

## When you step up I pause

today you stepped up for more
you headed out into the world
with anticipation
excited about your contribution
I had bad news
I chose to leave it
when you stepped back
I got a coffee
shared your excitement
then my bad news
corked for the day and ready to burst
one sentence
relief and despair

## Strike a light

lightning never strikes twice
that's what they say
that's crap I say
in every way
you cop hit after hit
first the brain
then massive pain
then there's another strike
body, brain, bum
hit, hit, hit, hit
none of it working — now you can't shit
like a lightning rod
in the peak of a storm
you attract and attract
how's that for form?

## Sigh

sigh, sigh,
living to die
sigh, sigh
living to die
sigh

## My punching bag

I have a punching bag
I punch it when I'm mad
I yell
I spit
push everyone away
the record stuck
exhausted, distorted
begging to rest
I belt my punching bag
my pillow and me

## Honey bun

today I ate a honey bun
loaded with cream
straight to my tum
the clouds are low
I just had to go
and leave you stewing
in your stew
desperate for instant indulgence
comfort
rumbling in my tum

## When you tell me

when you tell me about a problem
it overwhelms me and my day
please don't tell me

## Block of salt

they say they might be able to help
I phone
they say you have to contact them
you can lead a horse to water
you can't make it drink
where's the block of salt?

## 10 days in the bedroom

10 days in the bedroom
with the door closed tight
deep, deep black
wrapped in the arms of despair
love that embrace
take me there

## Circles don't work for me

get to the point
don't talk in circles
just say it
no convoluted conversations
just say it
no nuanced story
it's lost on me
my brain can't hold it all
just say it

## Help

want help
want it fast
scanned directory
got through at last
services – yes
only if he wants them – yes
you – you're doing great
keep going for walks
look after yourself
have a check up
take care
we're here for you


## Echo

she sat by the fire
in pain
and sighed
I wish the lord would take me
he did
60 years passed
he sat by the tv
in pain
and sighed
I'm living to die
I sigh
we are all living to die

## The owl

come into the dark he said
see the owl on the wall
been there an hour
being an owl

## Are you there?

instant succour
comfort food
constant fare
pantry bare
are you there?

## Salute to a GP

he's my doctor
I know he cares
he looks into my eyes
he takes time to explain
he acknowledges me
and shares my pain
he sees my state
he speaks plain
he cuts through jargon
I'm not a case
I think he sees himself in me
being human

## Replays

this chatter in my head
replays old news
it's current for me
don't you see?
I have no news
my world is small
spare me your big news
spare me your excitement please
battering my head and scraping my knees

## Small things with great love

today I watered pot plants
fed the fish
unloaded the dishwasher
big deal for me
small things with great love
and you took on the world

## You never come to Christmas

you never come to christmas
it's not that you don't care
you care so much
you care about what they think
you care about how they may judge
you care about losing your cool
you care about mucking up lunch
so you never come to christmas
does anyone care?
does anyone notice?
that ever empty chair

## Shadows

like a shadow
silently there
in your chair
if I step into my shadow
will you
step into your light

## Piggy in the middle

they meet you
you are eloquent
you look ok
so how do I explain what's going on
when you put on that smile
and say nothing

44

## Microwave brain

microwave brain going round and round
pounding pain
damn wire in my head
red rises
red blasting red
anger bouncing in my head
can't stop
firebrand torching
razor sharp
driven harpy
brain fried
surging tidal waves of pain
submerging consciousness again
you just don't get it
daggers in my head
please stop that microwave oven
please
you just don't get it
daggers in my head

## Diminished

we both agree
you're not a 'carer'
I'm not a 'caree'
sanitised, politicised, descriptors of love

## Surrender

surrender is an act of grace
no judgement in that hallowed space
simply be
simply be
simply be
no resistance in that hallowed space
it is as it is
it is as it is
it is

## I see you

I see you beyond your pain
I see you beyond your brain
I see you beyond your body
I see you in your heart
when you draw the blinds
I see you
swathed in constricting fear
I hear your silent murmurings
I hear your call for help
echoing
I see your struggle
as you move with stealth
I see your daily triumphs
as you unlock yourself

## Exile

this house is not my home
I will go to another place for a while
to give you a break
he said with a weary smile
I can't stay here
I feel stuck in this exile
I said with a weary smile
you're taking your bag to another exile

## Jocks and blocks

the 'jocks' on the radio
shocking again
lazy people not working
lazy people shirking
now to rock those 'jocks'
here's my truth
I want a life I want to work and I want everything you have
you jerk
a panel of experts all agree
I'm blocked for life
no go material with brain and body rocked
so here's to the 'jocks'
who haven't a clue about being blocked

## To those I love

if I seem selfish
it's because I'm trying so hard not to be
I have boundaries
but I'm not a victim
I'm doing the best I can
if I don't come to see you
it's not personal
if I fail to be there for you
remember my pain is taking all my energy
it's not about you


## Trading places

you slipped and fell
to a plastered arm
I cooked your meal
cut up your food
I felt I did something worthwhile
for you
I shifted my gaze
from my pain and my brain
I did something worthwhile for me

## *Illusion of permanence*

he was once a youth
handsome
when he smiled the room lit up
intellect sharp
commanding presence
with love on his arm
living the good life
without any qualm
everything ahead of him
he is older
still handsome
intellect sharp
commanding presence
emotions shackled
pain on his arm
living his best
everything ahead of him

## *Glimmers of joy*

the sun comes up
the sun goes down
a package of moments
little glimmers of joy
my nephews phoned and sang happy birthday
to this old boy shimmers of joy
innocence – no strings attached

## Loving kindness

caring for you
caring for me
caring for you caring for me
caring for me caring for you
loving kindness
doing the best I can do
she's getting older
he's getting older
a journey to completion
being the best I can be
loving kindness for you
loving kindness for me


## Acceptance

acceptance is not a dirty word
nor a statement of defeat
not anything heroic
not a victim's song
no big deal
acceptance is not giving up
acceptance is one moment at a time
acceptance is appreciation
acceptance is gratitude
acceptance is release
acceptance is being the best I can be
acceptance is another word for peace

# Acknowledgement

With deep appreciation to Ellen Sallows, whose art therapy classes
opened me up to writing poetry again.
Thank you to those who cared without concern and with respect and
acknowledgement held space for compassion.
Thank you to my cousin Ian Bidmeade, who inspired me with his poetry.
Special thanks to Bruce Bubner who generously provided the images for
this book.
I wish to thank my childhood friend Gail Schepel, who urged me to get
my poetry published. Our last precious hours together continue to fill me
with the peace and grace of acceptance.

# *About the Author*

Maureen lives on the south coast in South Australia with her son David.
She is the mother of two sons and a daughter and grandmother of five
young children.
After an extensive career in education she has established her own
business as a transition coach and mentor.

Maureen is co-author of a
of a published memoir *The Drive Home A New Map for Retirement.*

Her interests include reading, writing, long walks on the beach,
gardening, family history research and enjoying time with family and
friends.

Printed in the United States
By Bookmasters